DEC 1997

Read All About Numbers

NUMBERS AND SPORTS

John M. Patten, Jr., Ed.D.

The Rourke Corporation, Inc.
Vero Beach, Florida 32964

John M. Patten, Jr. Ed.D.
25 years of professional experience as a writer, elementary and secondary school teacher, elementary school principal and K-12 system wide director of curriculum.
    B.A.—English and social studies; M.ED.—Guidance and education; ED.D.—Education

MATH CONSULTANT:
Mrs. Barbara Westfield, M.S. — Grade Three Teacher

PHOTO CREDITS
All photos courtesy of Corel

Library of Congress Cataloging-in-Publication Data

Patten, J. M., 1944-
    Numbers and sports / by John M. Patten, Jr.
        p. cm. — (Read all about numbers)
    Includes index.
    Summary: Briefly explains the importance of numbers in sports to determine such things as the size of the play area, the length of the game, and the score.
    ISBN 0-86593-435-5
    1. Sports—miscellanea—Juvenile literature. [1. Sports—miscellanea.]
    I. Title II. Series: Patten, J. M., 1944- Read all about numbers
GV709.2.P66 1996
796'.021—dc20   96–12817
PAT   CIP
                                                                            AC

Printed in the USA

TABLE OF CONTENTS

WHAT'S THE SCORE?

Sports are for playing—running, jumping, swimming, throwing, kicking and catching. Numbers add a lot to games that make them fun to play.

Numbers tell the size of the play area, how long the game lasts and how many players are on each team. Numbers also tell the **score** (SKOR), or who is winning.

Let's read about some of the sports people play and the numbers that make the sports fun.

Team spirit, like numbers, is an important part of sports.

WATER POLO NUMBERS

Water polo is played in a swimming pool. Players cannot reach the bottom and must swim and float during the game.

Number of teams	2
Number of players	6 plus a goalie
Playing area size	90 feet by 60 feet
Goal size	10 feet by 3 feet

This water polo player is about to throw the ball at the goal.

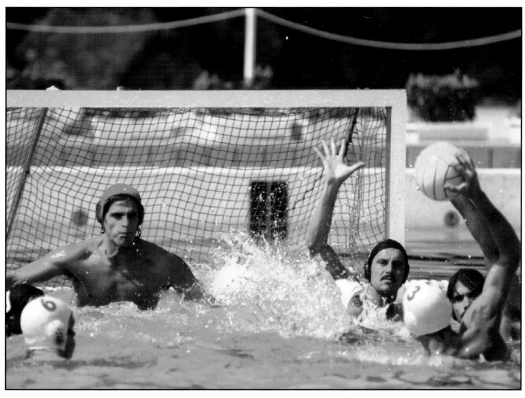

Water polo action—the goalie wears the red cap.

Players on each team try to throw a soccer-size rubber ball into the other team's goal.

Length of game	28 minutes
Number of periods	4 quarters, 7 minutes each
Scoring	1 point for each goal

Goalies may use two hands, but players may use only one hand to pass or shoot at the goal.

PLAYING BADMINTON

Badminton is similar in playing style and equipment to tennis.

Number of players	Singles - 2, doubles - 4
Playing area size	44 feet by 20 feet
Net	5 feet high
Racket size	26 inches long
Scoring	15 points to win

In badminton, one 3 $\frac{1}{2}$ ounce plastic or feather birdie is hit back and forth over the net. A point is scored when the birdie hits the ground or is out of bounds.

The birdie is in the air in this badminton match.

NUMBERS IN ICE HOCKEY

Ice hockey, fast and exciting, is played on a sheet of ice called a **rink** (RINGK).

Number of teams	2
Number of players	5 plus a goalie
Rink size	200 feet by 85 feet
Goal size	8 feet by 4 feet
Length of game	60 minutes
Number of periods	3, each 20 minutes
Scoring	1 point for each goal

The object of the game is to hit a hard rubber disc called a **puck** (PUHK) into the other team's goal. All players wear ice skates.

Ice hockey action around the goal.

PLAYING FIELD HOCKEY

Field hockey is played outdoors on grass.

Number of teams	2
Number of players	10 plus a goalie
Playing area size	100 yards by 60 yards
Goal size	12 feet by 7 feet

These players are controlling the ball in a field hockey match.

Chasing the ball in field hockey.

Players use curved sticks to try to hit a hollow 5-ounce ball into the other team's goal. No contact with other players is allowed.

Length of game	60 minutes
Number of periods	4, 15 minute quarters
Scoring	1 point for each goal

Field hockey is an exciting team sport played by both women and men.

SOFTBALL IS POPULAR

Softball is like baseball but the ball is larger, not as hard and always **pitched** (PITCHT) to the batter underhand.

Number of teams	2
Number of players	9 or 10
Bases	60 feet apart
Pitching mound	46 feet from plate (Men)
	40 feet from plate (Women)
Innings played	7

Softball is played two ways: slow pitch and fast pitch. This popular game is played by over 30 million people worldwide.

Pitcher in a softball game.

NUMBERS AND AMERICAN FOOTBALL

American football is played mostly in the United States and Canada. It is the favorite college and **professional sport** (pro FESH uh nel SPORT), or sport that pays players, in these two countries.

Number of teams	2
Number of players	11
Playing area	360 feet by 160 feet
Goal posts	18 feet high - 10 foot crossbar
Length of game	60 minutes
Number of periods	4, each 15 minutes

A touchdown counts 6 points; the kick after a touchdown is worth 1, and a run after touchdown is scored as 2. A field goal counts 3 and a safety 2.

The runners in the race must be at least 12 years old.

THE SPORT CALLED SOCCER

Soccer may be the world's most loved (and played) team sport. Millions play it in over 135 countries, trying to kick or head the ball into the other team's goal.

Number of teams	2
Number of players	10 and a goalie
Playing area size	130 yards by 100 yards
Goal size	24 feet by 8 feet

This player is heading the soccer ball toward the goal.

This soccer player is bringing the ball downfield.

The official soccer ball is air-filled and 28 inches around. Children use a smaller ball for their games.

Length of game	Up to 90 minutes
Number of periods	2, up to 45 minutes each
Scoring	1 point for each goal

Soccer's biggest event is called the **World Cup** (WURLD KUHP), played every four years by teams from hundreds of countries, out to prove who is the best.

HERE COME THE OLYMPICS

The first Olympic games were played over a thousand years ago. Today, the modern Olympics include both winter and summer **competition** (kom puh TISH en), or contests.

When played	Every 4 years
Where played	Selected host cities
Number of events	237 team and individual sport contests
Prizes	Gold (1st), Silver (2nd) and Bronze (3rd) medals

Our modern Olympic games are special for the **competitors** (kom PET uh terz)—those who actually play. The games are popular with **spectators** (SPEK tay terz) too—those who come and watch.

The Olympic flag—a symbol of the Olympic games.

GLOSSARY

competition (kom puh TISH en) — a contest

competitors (kom PET uh terz) — those who play in Olympic or other sport games

pitched (PITCHT) — thrown to the batter

professional sport (pro FESH uh nel SPORT) — sport that pays players

puck (PUHK) — hard rubber disc used in ice hockey

rink (RINGK) — ice hockey playing area

spectators (SPEK tay terz) — those who watch and cheer

score (SKOR) — tells who is winning

World Cup (WURLD KUHP) — soccer's biggest event

Platform diving is one of 237 Olympic events.

INDEX